EXTREMELY Weird ANIMALS

TARSIER

BY CHRISTINA LEAF

BELLWETHER MEDIA · MINNEAPOLIS, MN

Jump into the cockpit and take flight with *Pilot* books. Your journey will take you on high-energy adventures as you learn about all that is wild, weird, fascinating, and fun!

This edition first published in 2014 by Bellwether Media, Inc.

Library of Congress Cataloging-in-Publication Data

Leaf, Christina.
  Tarsier / by Christina Leaf.
    pages cm. – (Pilot. Extremely Weird Animals)
  Includes bibliographical references and index.
  Summary: "Engaging images accompany information about tarsiers. The combination of high-interest subject matter and narrative text is intended for students in grades 3 through 7"– Provided by publisher.
  Audience: Ages 7-12.
  Includes bibliographical references and index.
  ISBN 978-1-62617-079-7 (hardcover : alk. paper)
  1. Tarsiers–Juvenile literature. I. Title.
  QL737.P965L43 2014
  599.8'3–dc23
                        2013039593

Printed in the United States of America, North Mankato, MN.

TABLE OF CONTENTS

A MIDNIGHT SNACK

In the dark of night, the Indonesian **rain forest** is alive with sounds. High in a tree, a small, furry animal clings to a branch that reaches straight up to the starry sky. Its large ears constantly wiggle back and forth. Huge, goggling eyes stare into the darkness. Then, its neck swivels around so that its head almost completely faces backward. Its ears perk up and stop moving. The tarsier has heard something it likes.

Suddenly, the animal springs from one branch to another. Within a second of landing, the tarsier is holding a cricket with its long, thin fingers. It keeps watch by rotating its head back and forth while its sharp teeth munch on the cricket. As soon as the tarsier finishes its meal, it leaps off into the night to find something else to devour.

TINY PRIMATE

The tarsier is a small **primate** known for its enormous eyes and long hind legs. This tiny animal often measures between 4 and 6 inches (10 and 15 centimeters), and its tail usually grows to be around 8 to 10 inches (20 to 25 centimeters) long. It can weigh as little as 2 ounces (57 grams). However, most tarsiers weigh around 5 ounces (142 grams).

The tarsier spends much of its time in a crouched position. This means the tarsier's long hind legs often look shorter than they are. Its long tail is usually fully visible, though. Most species have hairless tails. Their tails do not have the thick gray or brown velvety fur that covers their bodies. However, some species have a little puff of hair on the tip of the tail.

human

tarsier

There are as many as 18 known species and **subspecies** of tarsiers in the world today. All live on islands in Southeast Asia. Scientists put them into three different groups depending on where they live. Western tarsiers live mainly on the islands of Borneo and Sumatra. The Indonesian island of Sulawesi hides eastern tarsiers in its thick forests. Just to the north, Philippine tarsiers make their homes on Philippine islands.

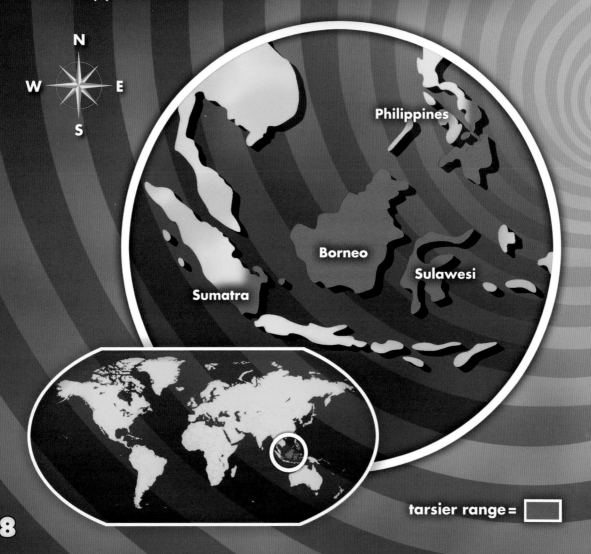

N
W   E
S

Philippines

Borneo

Sulawesi

Sumatra

tarsier range = ☐

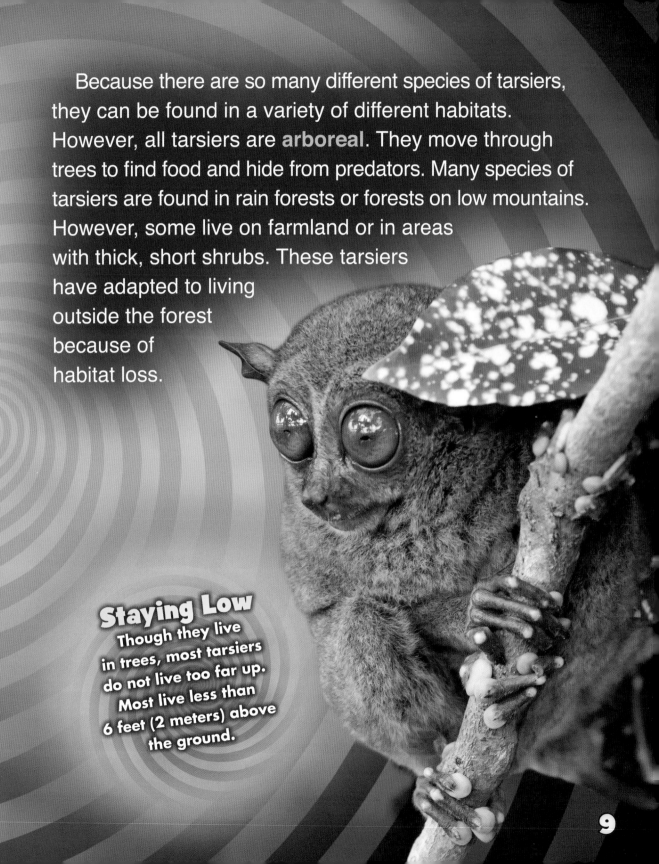

Because there are so many different species of tarsiers, they can be found in a variety of different habitats. However, all tarsiers are **arboreal**. They move through trees to find food and hide from predators. Many species of tarsiers are found in rain forests or forests on low mountains. However, some live on farmland or in areas with thick, short shrubs. These tarsiers have adapted to living outside the forest because of habitat loss.

Staying Low

Though they live in trees, most tarsiers do not live too far up. Most live less than 6 feet (2 meters) above the ground.

THE NIGHT LIFE

The tarsier's most noticeable feature is its bulging eyes. Just one of its eyes weighs more than its brain! The eyes are so big that they do not move in their **sockets**. They stare straight ahead. In order to look around, a tarsier uses its short, flexible neck. Like an owl, the tarsier can turn its head almost 180 degrees in either direction. This allows it to look almost anywhere.

The giant eyes allow tarsiers to see well at night. Their **pupils** expand in the darkness. This helps the tarsier see better by letting more light into the eye. The same thing happens with human eyes. However, human pupils are much smaller so they let in less light. Excellent night vision is important for tarsiers because they are **nocturnal** animals. They need to be able to find prey and see predators coming even in the darkest hour.

Wide-Eyed
Out of all the mammals, tarsiers have the biggest eyes for the size of their body.

Many nocturnal hunters have smaller eyes than the tarsier. Their eyes are smaller because they have a reflector in the back of their eyes. This reflector helps them see twice the amount of light in the darkness. These animals have **eyeshine**. Their eyes glow when light hits them.

Tarsiers do not have the reflector that most nocturnal animals have. This makes scientists think that tarsiers have not always been nocturnal. Some believe that tarsiers used to hunt during the day. Then they slowly switched to hunting at night. Over several generations, their eyes gradually grew bigger to adapt to this change.

eyeshine

Friendly Creatures

Tarsiers are also more social than most nocturnal animals. This supports the theory that they once were active during the daytime.

The tarsier's eyes are not the only features that help this small **mammal** at night. Tarsiers have **keen** hearing as well. Their large ears move independently of each other. When a tarsier is awake, its ears are always in motion. They wiggle around to help the tarsier hear sounds around the forest. When a tarsier hears something it likes, its ears can focus on that particular sound to pinpoint its meal.

These bat-like ears are sensitive enough to hear **ultrasonic** sounds. Most mammals, including humans, cannot hear ultrasonic sounds. Tarsiers use these high-pitched sounds to talk to one another without attracting predators. Insects such as moths and katydids also communicate with ultrasonic sounds. Tarsiers catch these insects by listening for them in the quiet of night.

JUMPING AROUND

While up in the trees, tarsiers must hang on tight. Long fingers and toes curl around the branches. Sticky pads at the tips of their fingers help them to grip the trees. They use their long tails to balance. They run their tails straight down the branch for support. Their tails have small ridges of skin to keep from slipping.

In 2008, scientists found three pygmy tarsiers. Everyone thought that they were extinct. They had not been seen since the 1920s!

Tarsiers leap through the air to travel around the forest. Their extremely long hind legs allow them to get around this way. Compared to the size of their body, these limbs are the longest of any mammal. Their legs are so long in part because of their unusually long **tarsal** bone. This anklebone earned the tarsier its name.

Lengthy Leaps

Tarsiers can jump 40 times their body length!

Tarsiers have other special traits to help them jump between the trees. Most animals have two separate shinbones on the lower legs. Near the ankle, the tarsier's shinbones join together. This acts as a **shock absorber** to make landing on a far off tree more comfortable. This is important because tarsiers often have to jump great distances. They can cover 6.5 feet (2 meters) in a single bound and leap nearly 5 feet (1.5 meters) up in the air!

Much of the time, tarsiers use their powerful legs to pounce on prey. They surprise their meal by landing directly on top of it. Sharp teeth help tarsiers tear apart their dinner. Tarsiers are the only primates that are totally **carnivorous**. They do not eat any plants.

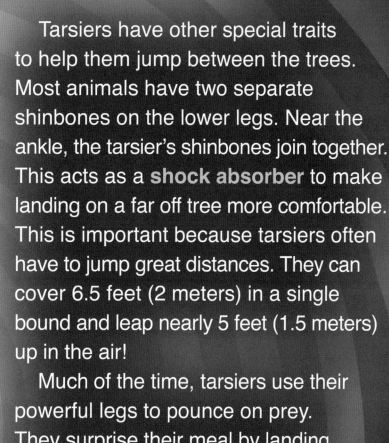

IN TROUBLE

All species of this tiny primate are decreasing in population. Some are already **endangered**. Tarsiers' biggest threat is humans. These little animals are losing their homes because of **deforestation**. Even thinned trees are a problem. The breaks in the **canopy** let in more moonlight. This makes it easier for predators to spot them.

Humans have also been impacting tarsiers more directly. Sometimes locals capture tarsiers and sell them as pets. People often go on tours to see tarsiers, which puts stress on the tiny primates. These little animals do not deserve such treatment. They help farmers by eating pests that harm crops. Their uniqueness also adds richness to the forests where they dwell. Humans need to protect tarsiers so they do not disappear from our Earth forever.

EXTINCT

EXTINCT IN THE WILD

CRITICALLY ENDANGERED

ENDANGERED

VULNERABLE

NEAR THREATENED

LEAST CONCERN

Tarsier Fact File

Common Name:	tarsier
Scientific Name:	Tarsiidae
Famous Features:	enormous eyes, long hind legs and fingers, bat-like ears
Distribution:	Brunei, Indonesia, Malaysia, the Philippines
Habitats:	mostly rain forests, some low scrubland or mountain forests
Diet:	mostly insects; sometimes small birds, frogs, or snakes
Life Span:	up to 16 years in the wild
Current Status:	depends on the species; all populations decreasing

GLOSSARY

arboreal—living or often found in trees

canopy—the covering of leafy branches formed by the tops of trees

carnivorous—only eats meat

deforestation—clearing an area of forests

endangered—at risk of becoming extinct

eyeshine—an effect when a nocturnal animal's pupils appear to glow

keen—sharp

mammal—an animal that has a backbone, hair, and feeds its young milk

nocturnal—active at night

primate—a member of a group of mammals that can use their hands to grasp food and other objects

pupils—the round, black parts of the eyes that let in light

rain forest—a thick, green forest that receives a lot of rainfall

shock absorber—something that absorbs the impact of a fall or jump

sockets—the spaces that hold eyeballs

subspecies—members of a species that are different from other members of the species due to their geographic range and certain physical characteristics

tarsal—a bone that makes up part of the ankle

ultrasonic—sounds that are too high of a frequency to be heard by a human ear

TO LEARN MORE

AT THE LIBRARY

Morgan, Sally. *Small Primates*. North Mankato, Minn.: Cherrytree Books, 2004.

Petrie, Kristin. *Tarsiers*. Edina, Minn.: ABDO Pub., 2010.

Shea, Nicole. *Creepy Mammals*. New York, N.Y.: Gareth Stevens Pub., 2012.

ON THE WEB

Learning more about tarsiers is as easy as 1, 2, 3.

1. Go to www.factsurfer.com.

2. Enter "tarsiers" into the search box.

3. Click the "Surf" button and you will see a list of related Web sites.

With factsurfer.com, finding more information is just a click away.

INDEX

The images in this book are reproduced through the courtesy of: BiosPhoto, pp. 5,
16-17, 17, 19; Stefano Paterna/ Alamy, pp. 6-7; Vitaly Titov and Maria Sidelnikova, p. 9;
Horoshunova Olga, p. 11; LOOK / Alamy, pp. 12-13; Mary Beth Angelo/ Getty Images,
p. 12; David Evison, pp. 14-15; Jurgen Freund/ Nature Picture Library, pp. 15, 18-19;
Efired, p. 21.